GEORGE FRID

C000066753

ZADOK THE PRIEST

Coronation Anthem

Edited by/Herausgegeben von
Damian Cranmer

Ernst Eulenburg Ltd

London · Mainz · Madrid · New York · Paris · Tokyo · Toronto · Zürich

© 1980 Ernst Eulenburg Ltd., London

All rights reserved. No part of this publication may be reproduced, stored in a retrieval system, or transmitted in any form or by any means, electronic, mechanical, photocopying, recording or otherwise, without the prior written permission of Ernst Eulenburg Ltd., 48 Great Marlborough Street, London W1V 2BN.

G. F. HANDEL
Coronation Anthems

The coronation of King George II and Queen Caroline took place on 11 October 1727 'with great magnificence, the queen being ablaze from head to foot with jewels, most of them hired'.[1] The music, no less splendid, fared better on originality, with Handel writing four new anthems for the occasion. But the details of the service are by no means clear and it is not certain that all happened as intended.[2] Against the anthem *The King shall rejoice* in his order of service, Archbishop Wake wrote 'The anthem in confusion, all irregular in the music'.[3] There is even doubt as to the order in which Handel's anthems were performed, and one account suggests that only three were played.

The names of several of the singers in this first performance are recorded in Handel's autograph score. At the beginning of *The King shall rejoice* the composer has written against the voice parts C[anto] 12, H[ughes] et 6, Freem[an] et 6, Church et 6, Wheely et 6, Gates et 6. This information is repeated four times in the same anthem, though not in any other. The first alto solos in *My heart is inditing* were to be sung by Hughes and Lee, the first bass solos by Wheely and Bell. However, the often quoted figure of 47 singers should perhaps not be taken as an exact record of the number in the choir at the coronation, being more likely a reflection of the composer's intentions before the event. Nevertheless, one contemporary account which not only corroborates the figure in general terms but also gives some insight into the relative size of choir and orchestra speaks of '40 voices, and about 160 Violins, Trumpets, Hautboys, Kettle-Drums, and Bass's proportionable'.[4]

Whatever the problems of the first performance of Handel's Coronation Anthems, their subsequent history has been illustrious, one or other appearing at every coronation since. If *Zadok the priest* has remained the favourite for these occasions, it must be because of the appropriate nature of its opening text: the music of the others is equally impressive. Handel himself was sufficiently pleased with the reaction to his anthems to advertise the first performance of the revised *Esther* in 1732 with the words 'The Musick to be disposed after the Manner of the Coronation Service'.[5] Indeed, *Esther* contains borrowings from two of the anthems. *My heart is inditing* is played complete at the end of Act I scene 1 and the first and last sections of *Zadok the priest* (that is omitting 'and all the people rejoiced', bars 31-62) form the finale to Act II. The opening of the latter anthem undergoes minor rhythmic changes to fit the words 'Blessed are all they that fear the Lord', but 'God save the king' remains unaltered.[6] Handel borrowed from the other two Coronation Anthems,

---

1 *Dictionary of National Biography*, vii, p. 1040
2 For a full discussion of the service see D. Burrowes: 'Handel and the 1727 Coronation', *Musical Times*, cxviii (1977), p. 469
3 Lambeth Palace Cod. Misc. 1079B, first discussed by W. Dean in a sleeve-note for the Argo record of the Anthems ZRG 5369
   Report of final rehearsal in O. E. Deutsch: *Handel: a documentary biography* (London, 1955) p. 215
5 O. E. Deutsch, op. cit. p. 289
6 The same two sections of *Zadok the priest* with the same new words were used for the final chorus of the *Occasional Oratorio*, 1746

along with several other works, for his next oratorio, *Deborah* (1733). At the end of Act I, the whole of *Let thy hand be strengthened* is introduced. The first two sections are separated by a recitative of thirty bars and both have different texts, obviously written by the librettist, Samuel Humphreys, to fit this music, which suggests that the borrowing was anticipated at an early stage of the preparation. The third section, 'Alleluia', concludes the act, but as Julian Herbage has pointed out,[7] it is a dramatic anticlimax and seems to have been included merely because of its position in the original work. The first section of *The King shall rejoice* ends Act II. Again new text was supplied, but although it had the same number of syllables as the original, the position of the stresses caused Handel to make some adjustments to the vocal parts, which he did by writing a new Bass part on a spare stave at the bottom of the autograph score of the Coronation Anthems and noting in the score of *Deborah* 'segue l'Anthem the King shall rejoice'. Two more sections of this anthem (bars 197 to end) form a large part of the final chorus of this oratorio. Rather more extensive revision of the vocal parts was necessary to fit the words 'O celebrate his sacred name, with gratitude his praise proclaim' to the music of 'Thou hast prevented him with the blessings of goodness, and hast set a crown of pure gold upon his head'. But the instrumental parts were left in their original form, causing discrepancies in the detail of the part-writing.

The Coronation Anthems continued to receive performances, several in conjunction with the Utrecht *Te Deum* and *Jubilate*. Entries in Deutsch[8] rarely refer to them individually but regularly as 'a Coronation Anthem', thus stressing the importance of their origin. They were published by Walsh in 1743 as 'Handel's Celebrated Coronation Anthems', a testimony to their continuing popularity, and exactly 100 years later they were chosen for the first volume of the short-lived English Handel Society.

The basis for the present edition is the autograph score in The British Library, though consideration has been given to several other sources. It can be assumed that the writing of this score was the final stage of composition. There are several instances of Handel changing his mind. The accompaniment figure at the beginning of *My heart is inditing* (bars 2, 4, 6 etc.) was originally preceded by another quaver which Handel has crossed out at each occurrence up to bar 50; where the figure reappears at bar 74 it no longer has the preliminary quaver. In *Zadok the priest* Handel originally wrote a bar between bars 65 and 66, identical to bar 64, but crossed this out, presumably before writing bars 103-5 where balance is restored by the reversal of 'God save the king' and 'Long live the king'. Handel's first idea for the final section of *The King shall rejoice* (bar 291) was for the Alto and Tenor to enter on the first beat of the bar; after writing four bars, he broke off and started again with the preliminary organ chord. There are also many changes in the scoring. For example, the semiquavers of bars 92-3 in *Zadok the priest* were originally written for Altos alone in thirds; in the final version the lower part is given to Tenors and first Basses. There are many other changes in the detail, some of which were introduced to tidy the part-writing or to remove parallel octaves or fifths,[9] while others seem to be the result of a change of mind. On the final

[7] G. Abraham, ed.: *Handel: a symposium* (London, 1954) p. 84
[8] O. E. Deutsch, op. cit.
[9] Some remain, see *Zadok the priest*, S II, A I and B I bb23-4 and S II and B I b28

leaf of *The King shall rejoice*, two plans survive. One is a single-line organ and bass part of bars 336-358 which continues in an ending different from the final version: the other is a sketch of the vocal parts of bars 328-336 in which, above a complete organ line, the entries of Bass I (bar 328 for one bar), Tenor (328, one and a half bars), Alto I (329, two bars) and Soprano (330, one bar) are noted on their respective staves. Perhaps plans such as these were the only written preparation for the writing of this autograph score. It might be illuminating to know the extent of Handel's involvement after the completion of this score, notably in the writing of the fair copies by J. C. Smith and his helpers, and in the printing of Walsh's published score. All contain some variant readings which, although not extensive, are significant.

Despite the extent of crossing out, the autograph score is very accurate, and for the most part easy to read. Some problems occur where Handel has altered a note by a 2nd, merely by enlarging the note-head, although he has often clarified these and other smudges by writing the letter name of the note in the space above the stave. As might be expected, the use of slurs, ties and trills is very inconsistent. As for the word-setting, where the texture is sufficiently homophonic, Handel has written the text in the Bass part only. Elsewhere, he generally gives enough information for his intentions to be understood, though there are relatively more problems in the alleluia sections. In places, the way in which the quavers are beamed together or left separate provides further information.

Handel uses C-clefs for Soprano, Alto and Tenor voice parts. In the continuo part, he uses four different clefs, which are significant, at least with regard to instrumentation. The bass clef implies 'tutti bassi' and the tenor clef 'senza contrabassi'. Where alto and soprano clefs are used, the bass instruments are not intended to play, and Handel has on occasions used 'senza bassi', not to be confused with 'senza contrabassi'. In the three C-clefs, the continuo part is written in two different ways: either a single line, a *basso seguente*, is figured to a greater or lesser extent and should be realized in the usual way, or there is an organ part in two or occasionally three parts. This is probably the complete organ part, indicating the actual notes to be played, rather than a mere guide or cue. These two methods of writing are not confused in Handel's manuscript, though they have been in later editions.

Barlines are drawn on the stave only, but in order to clarify the poor alignment Handel has periodically used long lines from top to bottom of the system; these often occur at four-bar intervals, though in some sections they are irregular Handel used eighteen-stave manuscript paper, which allowed him three staves for trumpets, one for timpani, two for oboes, three for violins, one for viola, seven for voices and one for the organ and bass instruments. For the opening of *Zadok the priest*, where there are independent lines for bassoons and organ, trumpets I and II share the top stave and oboes I and II the fourth. Where the texture is reduced for a complete section, Handel writes two systems to a page. In *The King shall rejoice* bars 75-189 are written in two eight-stave systems to a page, but the music runs along the top of two pages before going to the second system of the first page. There are two systems to a page in the section 'Kings' daughters' from *My heart is inditing* and throughout *Let thy hand be strengthened.* Since four staves are required for the strings and five more for the voices, there is no stave left for the oboes, which are indicated by directions such as 'Hautb. colla parte' or simply the letter 'H'. The oboe parts inevitably lose the independence which might have resulted from use of a different size of manuscript paper.[10] However, this limitation is unlikely to have worried Handel, a composer to whom meticulous detail was less important than a broad overall concept.

It is not surprising, therefore, that the Coronation Anthems provide several situations where editors have felt the need to 'improve' the detail. Bar 141 of *My heart is inditing* contains two such illustrations. On the third beat of the bar, the vocal parts have a chord of E with a suspended 4th, while the string parts have a six-four chord on E, that is concurrent 4th, 5th and 6th of the chord. The continuo figuring (4) follows the voices. Chrysander, who provided the basis for most modern editions, changed the Soprano minim b′ to crotchets c♯′ and b′, while leaving the Tenor minim b rather more difficult to 'correct', unchanged. It may not be insignificant that four bars later, where the same cadence occurs in the string parts alone, the continuo is figured $^6_4$.[11] The other point concerns the second note in the Bass, clearly g♯ in the autograph, both of the consulted early copies and Walsh's edition, but regularly changed to e to match the continuo. Arnold seems to have been the first to make this change. Examples such as this, of parts moving in unison or octaves but diverging for one note, are numerous. Some are obviously what Handel intended, while others have perplexed scribes and editors from the time of composition.

My thanks are due to the staff of the music libraries in The British Library, The Fitzwilliam Museum, Cambridge and The Central Library, Manchester for permission to consult manuscripts and for other assistance.

Damian Cranmer, 1980

---

[10] See the oboe parts of *My heart is inditing* bb142–6 which were written on the vacant soprano stave

[11] Two other examples of simultaneous but different cadences can be found in *The King shall rejoice* bb120 and 246

G. F. HÄNDEL

Coronation Anthems (Krönungskantaten)

König Georg II und Königin Caroline wurden am 11. Oktober 1727 gekrönt, ,mit grosser Pracht, die Königin von Kopf zu Fuss in Juwelen flammend, die grösstenteils im Verleih erhalten waren'.[1] Die nicht weniger prächtige Musik konnte sich eher rühmen, aus erster Hand zu sein, da Händel nicht weniger als vier neue Anthems für diese Gelegenheit geschrieben hatte. Es ist jedoch keineswegs klar, in welcher Weise der Gottesdienst ablief, und durchaus ungewiss, dass alles, wie beabsichtigt, erfolgte.[2] Der Erzbischof Wake schrieb in seiner Anordnung des Gottesdienst neben das Anthem *The King shall rejoice* ,das Anthem durcheinander, ganz unordentlich in der Musik'.[3] Sogar die Reihenfolge, in der Händels Anthems aufgeführt wurden steht nicht fest, und in einem Bericht wurde behauptet, dass es nur drei waren.

Die Namen einiger Sänger, die an dieser ersten Aufführung teilnahmen, sind in Händels Autographpartitur angegeben. Am Anfang des Anthems *The King shall rejoice* schrieb der Komponist vor die Gesangstimmen C[anto] 12, H[ughes] et 6, Freem[an] et 6, Church et 6, Wheely et 6, Gates et 6. Diese Angaben wurden viermal in demselben Anthem wiederholt, stehen aber in keinem anderen. Die ersten Altsolos in *My heart is inditing* sollten von Hughes und Lee, und die ersten Bass-Solos von Wheely und Bell gesungen werden. Die oft zitierte Anzahl von 47 Sängern dürfte jedoch vielleicht nicht als eine genaue Angabe der Grösse des bei der Krönung singenden Chors angesehen werden. Eher gibt sie, und das ist wahrscheinlicher, an, was sich der Komponist vor der Aufführung vorgestellt hat. Allerdings gibt es einen zeitgenössischen Bericht, in dem nicht nur diese Zahl im grossen ganzen beglaubigt wird, sondern der auch einen Einblick in das Zahlenverhältnis von Chor und Orchester gibt. Es steht dort, dass sich die Teilnehmer aus ,40 Stimmen, und ungefähr 160 Geigen, Trompeten, Oboen, Pauken, und Bässen im Verhältnis', zusammensetzten.[4]

Was auch immer die Probleme bei der ersten Aufführung von Händels Coronation Anthems gewesen sein mögen, ihre Geschichte, von diesem Zeitpunkt an, ist ruhmvoll gewesen, denn das eine oder andere dieser Werke ist seither bei jeder der folgenden Krönungen aufgeführt worden. Wenn *Zadok the priest* bei solchen Gelegenheiten der Vorzug gegeben wurde, so muss das daher kommen, dass der Text am Anfang so passend ist; doch ist die Musik der anderen Anthems nicht weniger eindrucksvoll. Händel war selbst so zufrieden

[1] *Dictionary of National Biography*, vii, S. 1040
[2] Für eine aufführliche Besprechung des Gottesdienstes vgl. D. Burrowes: 'Handel and the 1727 Coronation', *Musical Times*, cxviii (1977), S. 469
[3] Lambeth Palace Cod. Misc. 1079B, erstmalig von W. Dean in einer Beschreibung auf dem Plattenumschlag für die Argo-Platte der Anthems, ZRG 5369, besprochen
[4] Bericht über die letzte Probe in O. E. Deutsch: *Handel: a documentary biography* (London, 1955), S. 215

mit der Aufnahme der Anthems, dass er die Erstaufführung der überarbeiteten Fassung der *Esther* im Jahre 1732 mit den folgenden Worten ankündigte: ‚Die Musik ist nach der Art des Gottesdiensts bei der Krönung angeordnet.'[5] Tatsächlich hat er für *Esther* Musik aus zwei der Anthems entlehnt: *My heart is inditing* wird vollständig am Ende der ersten Szene im ersten Akt gespielt, und der erste wie auch der letzte Teil in *Zadok the priest* (d.h. mit Auslassug des ‚and all the people rejoiced', Takt 31-62) bilden zusammen das Finale des zweiten Akts. Der Anfang des letzteren Anthems wurde im Rhythmus geringfügig geändert, um mit den Worten ‚Blessed are all they that fear the Lord' übereinzustimmen, aber ‚God save the king' blieb unverändert.[6] Für sein nächstes Oratorium, *Deborah* (1733), borgte Händel Musik aus den beiden anderen Anthems, sowie aus einigen weiteren Werken. Am Ende des ersten Akts steht das ganze *Let thy hand be strengthened*. Zwischen den ersten zwei Teilen steht ein Rezitativ von dreissig Takten, und beide Teile haben einen verschiedenen Text, der offensichtlich von dem Librettisten Samuel Humphreys geschrieben wurde, um die Worte zu dieser Musik passend zu machen, was darauf hinzudeuten scheint, dass dieses Zurückgreifen auf die früher geschriebene Musik schon bei einem frühen Stadium der Vorbereitung geplant war. Der dritte Teil, ‚Alleluiah', beschliesst den Akt, stellt aber, wie Julian Herbage gezeigh hat,[7] dramatisch gesehen einen Abfall dar, und es scheint, dass er nur wegen seiner Einordnung im ursprünglichen Werk aufgenommen wurde. Der erste Teil des Anthems *The King shall rejoice* bildet den Schluss des zweiten Akts. Auch hier wurde ein neuer Text geliefert, doch obwohl er die gleiche Anzahl von Silben wie der ursprüngliche Text hatte, sah sich Händel durch die Stellung der Akzente gezwungen, die Gesangstimmen stellenweise zu ändern. Er tat dies, indem er eine neue Bass-Stimme auf ein freies unteres Notensystem in der Autographpartitur der Coronation Anthems schrieb und in der Partitur von *Deborah* angab: ‚segue l'Anthem the King shall rejoice'. Zwei weitere Teile dieses Anthems (Takt 197 bis zum Ende) bilden einen grossen Teil des Schlusschors in diesem Oratorium. Eine viel weitgehendere Revision der Gesangstimmen war nötig, um die Worte ‚O celebrate his sacred name, with gratitude his praise proclaim' der Musik des ‚Thou hast prevented him with the blessings of goodness, and has set a crown of pure gold upon his head' anzugleichen. Aber die Orchesterstimmen blieben in ihrer ursprünglichen Form, woraus im einzelnen Uneinheitlichkeiten in der Stimmführung entstanden.

Die Coronation Anthems wurden immer wieder aufgeführt, einige davon in Verbindung mit dem *Utrechter Tedeum* und dem *Jubilate*. Einträge bei Deutsch[8] erwähnen sie nur selten im einzelnen, aber regelmässig als ‚ein Coronation Anthem', wodurch die Bedeutung ihres Ursprungs betont wird. Walsh hat sie 1743 unter dem Titel ‚Handel's Celebrated Coronation Anthems' verlegt und damit einen Beweis ihrer anhaltenden Beliebtheit gegeben, und genau hundert Jahre später wurden sie dazu gewählt, in der Ausgabe der kurzlebigen englischen Händel-Gesellschaft den ersten Band zu bilden.

[5] O. E. Deutsch, siehe oben, S. 289
[6] Die beiden gleichen Teile in *Zadok the priest*, mit dem gleichen neuen Text, wurden auch für den Schlusschor des *Occasional Oratorio*, 1746, verwendet
[7] G. Abraham (Herausgeber): *Handel: a symposium* (London, 1954), S. 84
[8] O. E. Deutsch, siehe oben

Der vorliegende Ausgabe liegt die Autographpartitur zugrunde, die sich in der British Library befindet, doch verschiedene andere Quellen sind ebenfalls berücksichtigt worden. Es kann angenommen werden, dass die Niederschrift dieser Partitur das letzte Stadium des Kompositionsprozesses darstellt. In verschiedenen Fällen hat Händel seine Absicht geändert. Der begleitenden Figur am Anfang des Anthems *My heart is inditing* (Takt 2, 4, 6 usw.) ging ursprünglich noch ein Achtel voran, das Händel, überall wo es bis zum Takt 50 vorkommt, ausgestrichen hat; wo diese Figur im Takt 74 wieder auftaucht, steht sie ohne dieses vorangehende Achtel. In *Zadok the priest* schrieb Händel ursprünglich einen Takt, der zwischen den Takten 65 and 66 stand und mit Takt 64 identisch war, aber er strich ihn aus, vermutlich bevor er die Takte 103-5 schrieb, in denen das Gleichgewicht wieder durch die Vertauschung von ,God save the king' mit ,Long live the king' hergestellt wird. Händel hatte zunächst vorgehabt, den Schlussteil des Anthems *The King shall rejoice* (Takt 291) mit dem Einsatz von Alt und Tenor im ersten Taktteil dieses Taktes zu beginnen; nachdem er aber vier Takt geschrieben hatte, brach er ab und begann aufs neue mit dem vorangehenden Orgelakkord. Ausserdem stehen in der Partitur viele Änderungen in den Stimmen. So wurden, zum Beispiel, die Sechzehntel in den Takten 92-3 in *Zadok the priest* ursprünglich den Alt-stimmen allein in Terzen gegeben. In der endgültigen Fassung haben die Tenöre und die ersten Bässe die Unterstimme. Im einzelnen gibt es noch viele weitere Änderungen. Einige von ihnen betreffen die Verbesserung der Stimm-führung oder die Beseitigung paralleler Oktaven oder Quinten,[9] während andere anscheinend durch eine Änderung der Absichten des Komponisten entstanden sind. Auf dem letzten Blatt des Anthems *The King shall rejoice* haben sich zwei Entwürfe erhalten: Der erste ist eine einstimmige Orgel- und Bass-Stimme der Takte 336-358, die zu einem Ende geführt wird, das von der endgültigen Fassung verschieden ist; der zweite ist eine Skizze der Gesang-stimmen in den Takten 328-336, in welcher, über einer vollständigen Orgel-stimme, die Einsätze des B.I (Takt 328, für einen Takt), T. (328, 1½ Takte), A.I (329, 2 Takte) und S. (330, 1 Takt) auf ihren betreffenden Notensystemen notiert sind. Vielleicht waren derartige Entwürfe die einzigen aufgeschrie-benen Vorbereitungsarbeiten für die Niederschrift der Autographpartitur. Es könnte zur Erklärung einiger Fragen beitragen, wenn man wüsste, wie weit Händel nach Vollendung dieser Partitur noch an dem Werk beteiligt war, besonders in Beziehung auf die Reinschriften von J. C. Smith und seinen Helfern, sowie auf den Druck der von Walsh veröffentlichten Partitur. Alle enthalten gewisse Abweichungen im Notentext, die, wenn auch nicht weit-gehend, doch von Bedeutung sind.

Trotz der vielen ausgestrichenen Stellen, ist die Autographpartitur sehr fehlerlos und grösstenteils leicht zu lesen. Einige Probleme sind dort ent-standen, wo Händel eine Note durch Einzeichnen einer anderen änderte, indem er einfach den Notenkopf vergrösserte, obgleich er bei diesen und anderen verwischten Stellen oft den Buchstaben der Note in den freien Zwischenraum über dem Notensystem geschrieben hat. Wie zu erwarten, ist der Gebrauch von Bindungen, Bogen und Trillern sehr uneinheitlich. Was das Einsetzen der Worte betrifft, hat Händel den Text, dort wo der Satz homophon genug ist, nur in den Bass geschrieben. An anderen Stellen macht er, im

---

9 Einige sind geblieben, vgl. *Zadok the priest*, S. II, A. I und B. I, T. 23–4 und S. II und B. I T. 28

allgemeinen, seine Absichten verständlich genug, obwohl diesbezügliche Probleme im Alleluiateil verhältnismässig häufiger auftauchen. Dort, wo die Achtel entweder miteinander verbunden sind oder einzeln stehen, gibt er damit weitere Hinweise über seine Absichten.

Für Sopran-, Alt- und Tenorstimmen hat Händel C-Schlüssel verwendet. In der Continuo-Stimme hat er vier verschiedene Schlüssel benutzt, und diese sind von Bedeutung, wenigstens was die Instrumentation anbelangt. Unter dem Bass-Schlüssel soll man ‚tutti bassi' verstehen, unter dem Tenorschlüssel ‚senza contrabassi'. Wo Alt- und Sopranschlüssel stehen, sollen die Bass-instrumente nicht mitspielen, und gelegentlich schreibt Händel ‚senza bassi', was nicht mit ‚senza contrabassi' verwechselt werden darf. In den drei C-Schlüsseln ist die Continuo-Stimme auf zwei verschiedene Arten notiert: entweder ist sie eine Einzelstimme, ein mehr oder weniger bezifferter *basso seguente*, der in der üblichen Weise mit Akkorden zu versehen ist, oder sie steht als Orgelstimme in zwei oder manchmal drei Stimmen. Es handelt sich hier vermutlich eher um die vollständige Orgelstimme, in der die zu spielenden Noten angegeben sind, als um einen Leitfaden oder Hinweis für die Einsätze. Diese beiden Notierungsmethoden sind in Händels Manuskript deutlich geschieden, obwohl sie in späteren Ausgaben durcheiander gebracht worden sind.

Taktstriche erstrecken sich nur über die fünf Linien der einzelnen Noten-systeme, aber um die schlechte Ausrichtung dieser Taktstriche auszugleichen, hat Händel in Abständen lange Linien für das Gesamtsystem der Partitur eingezeichnet. Oft stehen diese Linien nach je vier Takten, aber in manchen Teilen der Partitur sind sie weniger regelmässig. Händel hat für sein Manu-skript ein Notenblatt mit achtzehn Liniensystemen verwandt, so dass ihm drei für Trompeten, eins für Pauken, zwei für Oboen, drei für Geigen, eins für Bratschen, sieben für Gesangstimmen und eins für die Orgel und die Bass-instrumente zur Verfügung standen. Im Anfang von *Zadok the priest*, wo Fagotte und Orgel selbständige Systeme haben, stehen Trompeten I und II auf einem, und zwar dem obersten System, und Oboen I und II auf dem vierten. Dort, wo die Instrumentierung in einem ganzen Teil der Komposition reduziert ist, benutzt Händel zwei Gesamtsysteme seiner Partitur auf einem Blatt. In *The King shall rejoice* sind die Takte 75-189 auf zwei solchen Gesamtsystemen, die aus je acht einzelnen bestehen, geschrieben, aber die Musik wird oben über zwei Seiten fortgeführt und geht erst dann auf das untere System der ersten Seite über. Auch bei dem Abschnitt ‚Kings' daughters' in *My heart is inditing* stehen zwei Gesamtsysteme auf einem Blatt, und ebenso durchgehend in *Let thy hand be strengthened*. Da für die Streicher vier Einzelsysteme und weitere fünf für die Gesangstimmen gebraucht werden, bleiben für die Oboen keine Systeme übrig, und diese sind daher durch Hinweise wie ‚Hautb. colla parte', oder einfach durch den Buchstaben ‚H' bezeichnet. Es ist unvermeid-lich, dass die Oboen deshalb die Unabhängigkeit einbüssen, die ihnen bei einem anderen Format des Notenpapiers vielleicht zugefallen wäre.[10] Jedoch hat sich Händel wohl darüber keine Sorgen gemacht, denn er war ein Kom-ponist, dem peinliche Genauigkeit im einzelnen weniger wichtig war als eine grosszügige Gesamtgestaltung.

[10] Vgl. hierzu die Oboenstimmen in *My heart ıs inditing*, T. 142–6, die ın das freie Notensystem des Soprans geschrieben sınd

Aus diesen Gründen wird es kaum überraschen, dass es in den Coronation Anthems mehrere Fälle gibt, bei denen es die Herausgeber nötig befunden haben, gewisse Einzelheiten in der Partitur zu ‚verbessern'. Takt 141 in *My heart is inditing* enthält zwei solcher Fälle. Im dritten Taktteil dieses Taktes singen die Stimmen einen E-Dur Akkord mit einer Quarte im Vorhalt, während die Streicher einen Quartsextakkord auf dem E spielen, wodurch Quarte, Quinte und Sexte im Akkord zusammenklingen. Die Bezifferung der Continuo-Stimme (4) folgt den Gesangstimmen. Chrysander, auf den sich die meisten neueren Ausgaben berufen, änderte die halbe Note h' im Sopran zu den Vierteln cis' und h', beliess aber dem schwieriger zu ‚korrigierenden' Tenor ein h' als halbe Note, ohne diese Stimme zu ändern. Es mag nicht ohne Bedeutung sein, dass vier Takte später, wo in den Streichern allein die gleiche Kadenz steht, die Continuo-Stimme mit $^6_4$ beziffert ist.[11] Der andere Fall betrifft die zweite Note im Bass. Im Autograph, in den beiden daraufhin untersuchten frühen Kopien und bei Walsh steht deutlich gis, das aber regelmässig zu einem e gemacht wird, damit diese Note mit der Continuo-Stimme übereinstimmt. Arnold scheint der erste gewesen zu sein, der diese Änderung vorgenommen hat. Derartige Fälle, bei denen die Stimmen im Einklang oder in der Oktave fortschreiten, aber in einer Note verschieden sind, kommen häufig vor. Einige sind offenbar von Händel beabsichtigt gewesen, während andere Gelehrte und Herausgeber seit Ursprung der Komposition aus der Fassung gebracht haben.

Ich möchte hiermit dem Personal der Musikbibliotheken der British Library, des Fitzwilliam Museums in Cambridge und der Central Library in Manchester für die Erlaubnis, die Manuskripte zu studieren, sowie für weiteren Beistand, meinen Dank ausdrücken.

Damian Cranmer, 1980
Deutsche Übersetzung Stefan de Haan

---

[11] Zwei weitere Beispiele von gleichzeitigen aber verschiedenen Kadenzen stehen in *The King shall rejoice*, T. 120 und 246

Editorial Notes

The numbering of the Anthems has been taken from the order in which they appear in the autograph, which is also that given in William C. Smith's Catalogue of Works.[12]

1. Zadok the priest
2. Let thy hand be strengthened
3. The King shall rejoice
4. My heart is inditing

Sources

AUT   British Library R.M. 20.h.5, autograph full score (1727). The score contains fifty manuscript leaves. The first twenty-five bars of Anthem 2, which are on f.11, are not in Handel's writing, having been added at some stage, presumably to make good a lost leaf. (Order of Anthems: 1, 2, 3, 4).

BL   Cambridge, Fitzwilliam Museum, Barrett Lennard Collection vol. 30, described as 'in the handwriting of his [Handel's] amanuensis John Christopher Smith'. This manuscript full score contains some interesting pencil ornamentation at the beginning of Anthem 4. (2, 1, 3, 4).

NF   Manchester, Central Library, Newman Flower Collection vol. 49. This is another manuscript full score written by one of the Smith copyists. At times various errors have been corrected. (2, 1, 3, 4).

WAL   'Handel's Celebrated Coronation Anthems in score for Voices and Instruments. Printed for J. Walsh...' (1743). This is the first published edition and although it contains a number or errors, it is a useful source. (1, 4, 2. 3, originally in separate volume, added at the end, unnumbered).

ARN   'Anthems for the Coronation of George II^D...' (c. 1795), published by Arnold as part of his projected complete edition of Handel's work. This is by far the least accurate of the scores consulted, but it is interesting, firstly for its attempt to translate some of the conventions of Handel's notation, and secondly as the source of many of the misprints which persist in modern editions. Arnold's numbering is confusing in that the numbers do not coincide with complete works. Thus although Anthems 2,1 and 4 are in a volume marked nos. 157-9, the number 157 is also given to the end of the previous volume containing *The King shall rejoice*, not the Coronation Anthem, but the anthem for the victory of Dettingen. Likewise, no. 159 continues into the next volume. Within the Coronation Anthem volume itself, Anthem 4 is partly no. 158 (up to bar 191) and partly no. 159. Anthem 3 is on its own in a volume marked nos.171-2. No.171 is also given to the end of *La Resurrezione*. (2, 1, 4. 3 separately).

[12] G. Abraham, ed.: *Handel: a symposium* (London, 1954) p. 275ff

CROTCH   'Anthems for the Coronation of King George II . . . printed for the members of the Handel Society MDCCCXLIII-IV'. This edition by Crotch has not been fully collated, offering as it does little more than corrections to Arnold, plus a few original errors. It is interesting that this score contains more added dotting than either ARN (1795) or HG (1863).

HG   'Krönungshymnen für König Georg II . . .' (1863), published for the Händel-Gesellschaft and edited by Friedrich Chrysander. It is surprising that Chrysander, who had access to the autograph score and the performing score in Hamburg, should so often follow errors first introduced by Arnold. Most modern vocal scores are based on this edition. (1, 3, 4, 2)

Square brackets are used for editorial additions, except for slurs and ties which are indicated by a vertical cross-stroke. Handel's accidentals apply only to the note itself and immediate repetitions. This method has been modernised by the omission of further accidentals in the same bar and by the addition of accidentals in subsequent bars. The cautionary accidentals are Handel's unless enclosed in round brackets.

Handel's timpani part has a key-signature throughout.

The soprano, alto and tenor clefs of these voice parts have been modernised, but the C-clefs of the Organ and Bass part have been retained (see Foreword). The figuring of the continuo part is from the autograph.

The spelling has been corrected and punctuation added.

Reference to obvious errors which occur in one source only have not been included in the commentary.

The pitch middle C is represented by c′, and the two octaves either side are indicated as follows: C-B, c-b, c′-b′, c″-b″.

ZADOK THE PRIEST

BARS	
1-30	ARN ties many of the organ notes together: bb1–2 (HG also), 3–4 (NF and HG also), 9–10, 11–12, 14–15, 16, 17, 21, 22
2	Ob I slurred (AUT)
12	Vl III, Vla slurs (AUT)
15	Vl I nn5,9 c♯′ (ARN, HG)
19	Vl I slurs (AUT)
23	Staccato dots for wedges (NF)
24	Timp nl minim (BL, WAL)
26–8	'annointed Salomon' (AUT, BL, NF)
30	Pauses in AUT vocal parts only
33–4	AUT and ARN have '-joi-ced', WAL '-joyc-d'. Did Handel intend the word to be three syllables here and two syllables in b36?
33	A II nn2–5 ♩. ♫ ♩ ; T nn3,4 ♫ ♩ (ARN)
35	Tr II nl ɤ· ♪ (HG), also Tr I, b37
49	Tr I nn1,2 equal quavers (ARN, HG); Handel's first idea ♫ ♫ ♫
52	Tr I nn3,4 ♩. ♪ (BL, NF, WAL, ARN), HG follows AUT
53	Tr I Handel's first idea ♫ ♫ ♫
55	A II, T last two notes ♩. ♪ (ARN)
56	Tr I nn1,2 ♩. ♪ (BL, NF, WAL, ARN, HG)
59	Tr II n2 a″ (ARN, HG)
60	Ob I ♩. Ob II ♩ ⅀ (WAL); Ob I, II ♩ ⅀ (BL)
65	Handel has crossed out a bat identical to b64 between bb65 and 66. This change of mind came before he wrote bb103–5 where there is no such extra bar and the order of the words is reversed.
65	Vl III n4 a′ (HG)
76	Vl II no tie (WAL, ARN)
85	T n4 c♯′ (HG and modern editions)
90	A II n8 e′ (WAL, ARN)
91	Vl I trill on n13 (HG)
108	Vl II no trill (WAL, ARN)
109	Tr I two tied minims (AUT)
111	B II n5 d (BL, WAL, ARN, HG), NF seems to have been changed from d to f♯
120	Tr II nn6 & 7 all sources have ♫ ♩ (ARN lacks tie). This results from a change in AUT. Handel's first idea for the trumpets in this bar was:

In Tr I & III the third and fourth beats were crossed out and rewritten, but in Tr II only the third beat was crossed out, a crotchet was written in front of the crossing-out and a tie added. Handel's intention was surely for the last note in this bar to coincide in all parts.

ZADOK THE PRIEST

G. F. Handel
1685-1759

EE 6681

2

8

re - joiced,   re - joiced,   re - joiced,

re - joiced,   re - joiced,   re - joiced,

re - joiced,   re - joiced,   re - joiced,

re - joiced,   re - joiced,   re - joiced,

re - joiced,   re - joiced,   re - joiced,

12

14

EE 6681

Long live the king!
Long live the king!
Long live the king!
Long live the king!
Long live the king!
Long live the king!
Long live the king!

May the king live for e - ver, a-men, a-men, al - le - lu - ia, al - le -
May the king live for e - ver, a-men, a-men, al - le - lu - ia, al - le -
May the king live for e - ver, a-men, a-men, al - le - lu - ia, al - le -

A-men, a-men, al - le - lu - ia, al - le -
A-men, a-men, al - le - lu - ia, al - le -
A-men, a-men, al - le - lu - ia, al - le -

Vc. e Fg.
Tutti
Organo tasto solo

87
I
Tr. II
III
Timp.
I
Ob.
II
I
Vl. II
III
Vla.
S.
- men. May the king live for e - ver, for e - ver, for
A. I
May the king live, may the king live for e - ver, for e - ver, for
A. II
May the king live, may the king live for e - ver, for e - ver, for
T.
May the king live, may the king live for e - ver, for e - ver, for
B. I
May the king live, may the king live for e - ver, for e - ver, for
B. II
May the king live, may the king live for e - ver, for e - ver, for
Org. e Bassi

112